MARCH WINDS AND APRIL SHOWERS

MARCH WINDS
and
APRIL SHOWERS

Country Weather Lore

Ralph Whitlock

EX LIBRIS PRESS

Published in 1993; reprinted 1995 by
Ex Libris Press
1 The Shambles
Bradford on Avon
Wiltshire

Typeset in 10 point Palatino

Design and typesetting by Ex Libris Press

Cover printed by Shires Press, Trowbridge
Printed and bound in Great Britain by
Cromwell Press Ltd., Broughton Gifford, Wiltshire

ISBN 0 948578 53 X

This book is illustrated throughout with engravings by
Thomas Bewick, 1753-1795. There is a human and endearing
quality in every Bewick woodcut and it is a joy to have the
opportunity of using a small selection of his vast output in
these pages. Thankyou, Thomas – *Editor*
The illustrations are taken from *1800 Woodcuts by Thomas
Bewick and his School* (Dover Publications, 1962)

CONTENTS

INTRODUCTION

LIFE FOR OUR ANCESTORS had as its horizons the hedges of the village fields. In those fields they ploughed and hoed and harvested. Along the village lanes they drove their cows and sheep to pasture. In the woods they gathered nuts and firewood and set their pigs foraging for acorns. On the moors and downs beyond the limits of cultivation they watched their sheep grazing through the short summer months.

Because they had no artificial illumination, other than candles and rush-lights, they went to bed early and rose early. Working hours, except at the height of summer, were from sunrise to sunset, or in some instances from half-an-hour before sunrise to half-an-hour after sunset. Sunday was a holiday, but every one was expected to attend church. There was, indeed, nowhere else to go. Once or twice a year, perhaps, the villagers would walk to the nearest town, several miles away. Their visits would generally coincide with a fair, but many villagers, particularly the women, did not even get that break from routine.

Confined within such narrow limits, they had to find their pleasure in the context of their work programme. Fortunately, the cycle of farm life produces its own natural seasons for festivity. Seedtime and harvest come round as regularly as day and night. So, too, do haymaking, sheep-shearing, the mating of sheep, the autumn killing of surplus animals for which there will be insufficient food in the coming winter, and the midwinter festival when the day is at its lowest ebb.

There are, in fact, two natural rural calendars, namely, an agricultural and a pastoral. The agricultural is illustrated by the still extant quarter days – Lady Day (March 25th), Midsummer (June 24th), Michaelmas (September 29th) and Christmas

(December 25th). The pastoral, which is much older, is represented by the old Celtic quarter days, which are Imbolc (February 1st), Beltane (May 1st), Lugnasad (August 1st) and Samhain (November 1st).

This pastoral calendar has largely lost its identity through being submerged by the later agricultural calendar, but the old feast days have been taken over and remembered under different names. Imbolc, which was a lambing festival, has become Candlemas Day; Beltane is still synonymous with May Day; Lugnasad has been transposed into Lammas-tide, the festival of the first-fruits; Samhain has become Martinmas, though with a greater emphasis being placed on its Eve, which is, of course, Hallowe'en.

The agricultural calendar was in due course overtaken and Christianised, the medieval ecclesiastical calendar being overwhelmed by a plethora of saints' days. Nevertheless, the composite calendar served its purpose very well, though its threads need considerable unravelling before we can understand why a certain festival was held on a certain date. It enabled a conservative peasantry to keep up their old festivals at the traditional times without offending the priest. And the multiplicity of saints' days seemed a providential arrangement for giving hard-worked country folk an adequate number of holidays – bearing in mind that holidays were, in their origin, 'holydays'.

The essence of a rural festival is that it serves a practical purpose. Most modern revivals of ancient customs qualify in that respect, for most of them are concerned with the very practical aim of raising money for some worthy local cause. Our ancestors had a sure instinct for holding on to anything that served a practical purpose, and we have not entirely lost it.

The manipulation of the calendar in the year 1752 produced some rather awkward anomalies, apart from the near-riots by simple folk who thought they were being robbed of eleven days of their lives. The situation arose, of course, through an error

in the Julian Calendar, which was adopted by most western European countries from the sixth century AD onwards. The equinoctial year does not lend itself to simplification, for it contains an awkward fraction in that it comprises 365.2422 days. The Julian Calendar attempted to deal with that fraction by making every fourth year a leap year, of 366 days. This helped, but the devisers of the Julian Calendar were trapped into error by applying the rule to *every* fourth year. They should have excluded the last year of a century, except when the year is divisible by 400. Thus, the year 1600 would be a leap year, but the year 1700 would not.

By the sixteenth century the error amounted to ten days.

What should, according to the original calculations, have been March 11th was now March 21st. Accordingly in 1582 Pope Gregory XIII introduced what has ever since been known as the Gregorian Calendar. Ten days were dropped, to eliminate the accumulated error, and from henceforward leap years were dealt with in the proper manner.

Most of the Catholic countries adopted the new style of reckoning in that year of 1582, and most of the rest of Europe followed in 1583. But Protestant England would have nothing to do with it until 1752. By then the error had grown to eleven days, which were accordingly sliced from the calendar between September 3rd and 14th of that year.

The change gave rise to considerable confusion and controversy. Ought the dates of certain traditional events to be calculated according to the old or new calendar? A good test case seemed to be offered by the West Country custom of wassailling the apple-trees. Apple orchards were traditionally wassailled on the Eve of Twelfth Night, the twelfth night after Christmas, which was by the old reckoning January 4th. But if the calendar had not been tampered with, Twelfth Night would still be January 5th, whereas by the new reckoning it would be January 16th. Which date was the correct one?

Seeking a sign, great crowds gathered at Glastonbury at Christmas (new date) 1753, to see what the sacred thorn would do. Local tradition asserted that the thorn was a descendant of one which had sprung from the staff of Joseph of Arimathea when he brought the Christian gospel to Somerset within a few decades of the Crucifixion. It had the reputation of always coming into bloom on Christmas Day, and, indeed, in 1645 a clergyman, Rev. John Eachard, quoted the fact as proof that December 25th was Christ's birthday. So the crowds assembled to see whether the thorn would adapt itself to the new Calendar. It did not. No blossoms appeared until January 16th, which was the appropriate date when the loss of the eleven days had been allowed for. Nature and supernature were obviously adhering to the old calendar, and a wise man would follow their example.

JANUARY

January begins with a largely forgotten festival, Twelfth Night. The Christmas holiday traditionally extended for twelve days after Christmas, during which no work was to be done. That, however, depended on the definition of 'work'. Cows had to be milked, sheep and cattle fed and watered, cattle-sheds cleaned out, hens fed, and a score of other chores tackled around the farm. 'Work' therefore meant 'work in the fields', which at this season consisted chiefly of ploughing. And the institution of Plough Monday, when the plough was taken to church and blessed by the priest, had the effect of extending the holiday by yet another day! In some places men with blackened faces, after attending church, paraded around the village, asking for alms and threatening to plough up the doorstep of any householder who refused. The money thus collected was used for buying beer in an evening of dancing and revelry.

January has its quota of weather lore:

> *A snow year, a rich year.*

> *If in January you sow oats,*
> *it will bring you golden groats.*

January would be unusually early for sowing oats or anything else, but any crops sown would be getting a flying start, if they survived.

> *The blackest month in all the year*
> *Is the month of Janiveer.*

> *If the grass looks green in Janiveer*
> *Twill look the worser all the year.*

There are a number of weather sayings with the same import. Thus:

> *March in Janiveer,*
> *Janiveer in March, I fear.*

> *In January should sun appear,*
> *March and April will pay full dear.*

> *A January spring is good for nothing.*

> *A warm January, a cold May.*

> *January blossoms fill no man's cellar.*

> *A green January, a full churchyard.*

The message is straightforward. Warm weather in January encourages crops to become too forward and therefore liable to be damaged by subsequent frost. Unfortunately there is no truth in this weather lore. At the time of writing we have just enjoyed a virtually frost-free January, and it was followed by two mild winter months and then heat-waves and drought in April, May and June.

> *As the days lengthens, so the cold strengthens.*

is usually correct, however.

> *Much rain in January, no blessing to the fruit,*

and

> *Is January wet? The barrel remains empty,*

are proved erroneous in recent years. My apple trees are bearing well this summer, in spite of a mild January, though the January rainfall was less than usual.

Certain saints' days in January have their share of weather prognostications:

> *If the sun shines on January 12th (which is Plough Monday) it foreshadows much wind.*

And then St. Vincent's Day (January 22nd):

> *Remember on St. Vincent's Day,*
> *If the sun his beams display,*
> *Be sure to mark his transient beam*
> *Which through the casement sheds a gleam;*
> *For 'tis a token bright and clear*
> *Of prosperous weather all the year.*

But our ancestors paid even greater attention to the weather on St. Paul's Day (January 25th):

> *If St. Paul's Day be fair and clear*
> *It doth betide a happy year.*
> *But if, by chance, it then should rain,*
> *It will make dear all kinds of grain,*
> *And if the clouds make dark the sky,*
> *Then neate and fowls this year shall die.*
> *If blustering winds do blow aloft,*
> *Then wars shall trouble the realm full oft.*

Here the weather on St. Paul's Day is held to influence national and political events, including war.

The confusion over the calendar extended right through January. Those who held to the old style celebrated Christmas on January 6th, of which it was said:

> *If the sun shines before twelve o'clock on Old Christmas Day there will be an abundance of apple-blossom and fruit during the year. And if the sun shines through the apple-trees on that day it will be a good cider year.*

Old Christmas Day was held to be a horse's holiday, when no owner would allow a horse to be taken out of his stable. Anyone who rides or drives on that day is certain to meet an accident. If old Christmas Day came during a waxing moon a good year would follow; but if during a waning moon a hard year was forecast. The nearer the end of the moon, the worse were the expectations.

FEBRUARY

Although February is the shortest month of the year it yields to none in the matter of weather lore. Perhaps the best known appellation is 'February Fill-Dyke', testifying to the need for the soil to be thoroughly soaked in February:

> *If it rains in February every day,*
> *In June you're sure of plenty of hay.*

is accurate enough. Another version is:

> *February fill ditch,*
> *Black or white, don't care which.*

This refers to the form taken by precipitation, black being rain and white snow. But an addition says,

> *If it be white*
> *Tis better to like.*

Countrymen have learned to beware of a mild February:

> *A February spring is not worth a pin.*

says one, while another asserts that when gnats dance in February the husbandman becomes a beggar.

February is in general raw, damp and unpleasant, but it sees the first signs of spring. Snowdrops and crocuses are among the earliest spring flowers and birds choose their mates, while some start nest-building.

In some districts the first snowdrops are associated with Candlemas Day, February 2nd. Candlemas Day, of course, is a festival devoted to the Purification of the Virgin Mary, observed in the Roman Catholic Church by the carrying of candles by a mother on her first visit to a church after childbirth, but it happened to coincide with the Celtic feast of Imbolc, a lambing festival. Even now the first week of February is the time when many farms start lambing. Although in the depth of winter and requiring special provision to be made for the shelter of ewes and lambs, the early date offers two considerable advantages. One is that the lambs are just the right age to make good use of the spring grass as soon as it is available; the other, that the lambs are well-grown and ready to catch the lucrative market for them in June and July.

Much of the Candlemas weather is admonitory:

> *In the barn on Candlemas Day*
> *Should be half the straw and half the hay.*

Some versions say 'half the straw and two-thirds the hay' but the message is the same. In spite of signs of the approach of spring, winter should be reckoned as to be no more than half over. Half the winter livestock rations should be untouched. However, there is a weather saying to fit the occasion:

> *If Candlemas Day be fair and fine*
> *Half the winter is left behind;*
> *If Candlemas Day be dull and gloom,*
> *Half the winter is yet to come.*

On the other hand,

> *If Candlemas Day be cloudy and black*
> *Twill carry cold winter away on its back;*
> *But if Candlemas Day be fine and clear,*
> *Then half the winter's to come this year.*

We must take our choice from these two diametrically opposed proverbs. The warnings are reinforced by:

> *If the sun shines on Candlemas Day hard frost is sure*
> *to set in.*

And:

> *As much ground as is covered with snow on*
> *Candlemas Day will be covered with snow before*
> *Lady-Day.*

Also it is generally believed that if we have bright sunshine on Candlemas Day we can look forward to a plentiful snowfall ere long.

When the wind's in the east on Candlemas Day,
There it will stick to the 2nd of May.

Well, there's often a spell of north-easterly winds in late winter, but this proverb is not infallibly true.

Sow oats when the parson begins to read Genesis,

is a saying that probably requires a little explanation. February 1st is Septuagesima Sunday, on which day, according to old tradition, the lesson for the day was Genesis, Chapter One.

And superstition has it that unless every vestige of Christmas decoration is cleared away before the Eve of Candlemas there will be a death in the family occupying the pew where this precaution is neglected. But there is a qualifying proverb which enjoins:

Kindle the Christmas Brand and then
Till sunne-set let it burne,
Which quencht, then lay it up again,
Till Christmas next returne.
Part must be kept wherewith to tend
The Christmas Log next years.

In old times when the holly and the ivy were taken down, on the Eve of Candlemas Day, they were replaced by box (which in its turn was replaced at Easter by yew).

When the elm leaf is as big as a mouse's ear
Sow your barley without any fear,

is a proverb which it is impossible to put to the test, since Dutch elm disease made a clean sweep of all our elm-trees, but I would have thought that Candlemas was a bit early for elm to have leaves on that size. However, the belief that beans should be sown or set by Candlemas is probably sound enough.

There are a number of proverbs to the effect that,

> *By Candlemas Day every good goose or duck ought*
> *to lay.*

And there is much homely wisdom in the advice:

> *Plant raspberry canes on Lord Mayor's Day*
> *[November 9th]*
> *And cut them down for their first year on*
> *Candlemas Day.*
>
> *Apples, pears, hawthorn, oak, set them at All*
> *Hallow-tide and command them to prosper; but set*
> *them at Candlemas and entreat them to grow.*

This gives the ideal dates for planting those trees. Planting them at Hallowe'en is the ideal time, but Candlemas is the latest possible date and even then you have to 'entreat' them to grow!

In the saying

> *At New Year's Day, a cock's stride;*
> *At Candlemas, an hour wide,*

the allusion is to the gradual lengthening of the days.

> *On Candlemas Day, high or low,*
> *Out the candles we must blow,*

and it was regarded as an evil omen if the candles began to splutter.

Of the proverbs that are sprinkled throughout February a pleasant one, though without much significance, is:

> *If by the 10th the snowdrops are out,*
> *More snow throughout the month without a doubt.*
> *If the sun shines on St. Eulalie's Day,*
> *Tis good for apples and cider, they say.*

Needless to say, this is a Somerset proverb, with its concern for the apple crop.

St. Valentine's Day, halfway through February, is primarily concerned with courtship:

> *This is the day birds choose their mate,*
> *And if I choose you, if I'm not too late.*

There is, however, one piece of weather lore associated with the day:

> *If Valentine's Day be bright and fine,*
> *Half the winter is left behind.*

And it was frequently held that 'Valentine's Day broke the back of winter.'

Shrove Tuesday is a movable feast, controlled by the date of Easter. Easter Day is the first Sunday after the first full moon on or after March 21st. The forty days before are known as Lent, and Lent is preceded by Shrove Tuesday. All of these church festivals and their religious significance were familiar to our rural ancestors and may well have meant more to them than to us.

Lent was traditionally a period of fasting, or at least of abstinence from certain foods and pleasures. Shrove Tuesday therefore provided the opportunity for a last fling before the austerity of Lent. Devout folk considered it necessary to use up any foodstuffs which were forbidden during Lent, which certainly included meat and, according to some authorities, eggs and butter as well. That does not appear very logical, as eggs would seem to be one of the few commodities the supply of which tends to increase with the advent of spring, but the practice could have been an indirect method of ensuring a good hatch of chicken for the ensuing year.

Shrove-tide is thus a jolly festival, a preparation for the gloom of Lent. It is Pancake Day, when eggs galore were used up to make a feast. It is also 'Lentshard Day', a ceremony involving the smashing of lots of crockery. Egg shackling, which involved shaking eggs gently in a sieve to see which one would stay unbroken longest; thrashing the hen and other ingenious rustic sports. But, as it wandered about the calendar, it failed to attract any weather lore.

February fades away without any further noteworthy occasions. If it freezes on St. Matthias-Day the frost will continue for a month, but who, without a reference book, knows that St. Matthias-Day is February 24th? A pseudo-practical tip is to plant broad beans on the first day on the new moon in February – the reason: to prevent attacks by the dolphin aphis!

Farmers and shepherds are said to maintain that a leap year is a bad sheep year – a poor year for lambs.

MARCH

In England all months are capricious, but March is most fickle of them all. Often a cold winter extends its sway well into March, and even if the month be mild there will be sure to be an Arctic spell before it ends. Yet an unfailing feature of it is a foretaste of spring, even summer. At some time, usually in the middle of the month, the wind shifts to south and for a few days brings warm air from the Mediterranean, coaxing the opening of the spring flowers. The respite is soon over, and winter returns as rigorously as ever, but it has left its mark. No matter that the north-east wind brings frost and snow, we have had a taste of spring and know that before long the warming sun will have its way.

March is, if anything, a windy month and

> *March winds and April showers*
> *Bring forth May flowers.*

Though a warning is sounded by the proverb

> *When March is like April,*
> *April will be like March.*

March is the great sowing month, when dry weather is at a premium, so

> *A peck of dust in March is worth a king's ransom.*

For a farmer to get most of his grain sown in March ensured that he was halfway to a good harvest.

> *Dust in March brings grass and foliage*

and

> *A dry and cold March never begs for bread.*

In the same vein is the saying:

> *March rain spoils more than clothes.*

And there is a good deal of credence to be placed on the proverb:

> *If March comes in like a lion it goes out like a lamb,*

and vice versa. Likewise,

> *So many fogs in March, so many frosts in May,*

which is approximately correct, by the law of averages.

> *A dry March fills barn and cellars and brings much hay,*

falls into the same category as

> *A March without water dowers the hind's daughter,*

emphasising the importance placed by our rural ancestors on a good sowing season.

For some reason, the significance of which is lost, a Saturday moon in a month foretells a series of disasters:

> *A Saturday moon,*
> *If it comes once in seven years*
> *Comes too soon.*

And its appearance on the first night that a new moon is visible indicates the sort of weather that may be expected during the coming month. If it is 'on its back' a stormy month will follow, but if you can see a three-day old moon clearly that denotes fine weather.

When home-brewing was widespread, March was the brewing month, and March beer was noted for its excellence. In those days beer was often kept for a year before drinking, and frequently for two years or more, by which time it was pretty strong stuff.

March was also the month for hedge-laying, on the principle that a hedge shaped in March had all the year to grow into the proper shape. According to tradition, this task should always be undertaken in 'the growing of the moon'. Besides this, the points of the laid saplings should, if possible, point towards the sun, 'as they will grow better and spread more', which seems sound reasoning. As regards the sowing of seed in general, this should be done while the moon is waxing, except for beans, which are sown during a waning moon, but why the different treatment I have never been able to ascertain. Some versions include onions as seeds to be sown 'in the shrinking of the moon'.

March has three saints' days at the very beginning of the month – St. David's on March 1st, St. Chad's Day on March 2nd, and St. Winwaloe's Day on March 3rd. St. Winwaloe is of little account in any hagiography and is remembered only because he makes up the trio. St. Chad has a couple a couplets to commemorate him. One is an exhortation not to delay the sowing of peas any longer:

> *David and Chad,*
> *Sow peas, good or bad.*

And the other reminds us that

> *Before St. Chad*
> *Every goose lays, both good and bad.*

St. David's Day provides an attractive example of good neighbourliness. In old-time villages if any small farmer or peasant had, through illness or misfortune, failed to get his land ploughed by the date, his neighbours rallied round to help him. They came to the farm with their ploughs and oxen, and accompanied by their wives who cooked for the entire company. As food was scarce by that time of the year, leeks (for which St. David's Day is noted) were a welcome addition to the communal stock-pot, and every housewife brought her quota.

Another minor celebration of St. David's Day was the sweeping of the front doorstep on the early morning to prevent an invasion by 'The Black Army'! These were fleas! An old rhyme records:

> *Keep your windows close tight,*
> *Else the fleas will come in and bite.*

The inference is that at this time of the year fleas awoke from hibernation and became active, and I suppose there may have been some truth in the conjecture. But it occurs to me that St. David's Day is very nearly Lady Day, when farms and farm-workers changed hands. One can imagine that in the general post that went on the countryside around that date the fleas would be subjected to a wholesale disturbance of the snug quarters where they had spent the winter and so went in search of new lodgings.

There are few other saints' days of any consequence in March. Mothering Sunday, which falls midway in Lent, is a movable feast and therefore cannot have attracted much weather lore, though it has become the repository of a number of interesting customs. The weather on Old St. Matthew's Day (March 8th) is said to indicate, or even influence, the weather for the rest of the month. An interesting point about this tradition is that it refers to *old* St. Matthew's Day, an example of the tenacity of a ruling which came to an end with the adoption of the new calendar in 1752.

St. Patrick's Day falls on March 17th but his memory is eclipsed in the West Country by that of St. Joseph of Arimathea, around whom a good deal of traditional lore has accumulated. The one piece of weather lore which has survived says:

> *If St. Joseph's Day is clear,*
> *We shall get a fertile year.*

Lady Day (March 25th) was widely recognised as the day when both indoor and outdoor servants made a year's agreement with their employers that they would not change their situation during the following year. If notice were not given it was assumed that the employee was content and would remain till the end of the coming year.

I have one piece of weather lore to record:

> *An east wind on Lady-Day*
> *Will keep on till the end of May.*

On Lady Day the lady's smock or cuckoo-flower generally comes into bloom, and naturalists look eagerly for the first cuckoo (though they are often disappointed, for the cuckoo normally does not put in an appearance until April). The chiffchaff, however, is usually heard uttering its monotonous little note in the last week of March, and the wheatear and stone-curlew arrive on migration, though both have now become scarce. Rooks are busy at their nests, and the first blackbird and thrush eggs are found. In the woods primroses, wood anenomes and bugle are in full bloom, while the countryman who finds his boot can cover nine daisies at once argues that spring has arrived.

Here may be a convenient place to quote the 'Signs of Foul
Weather', as recorded by one Dr. Jenner:

The hollow winds begin to blow;
The clouds look black, the glass is low;
The soot falls down; the spaniels sleep,
And spiders from their cobwebs peep.
Last night the sun went pale to bed;
The moon in haloes hid her head.
The boding shepherd heaves a sigh,
For see, a rainbow spans the sky.
The walls are damp; the ditches smell;
Closed is the pink-eyed pimpernel.
Hark! how the chairs and tables crack;
Old Betty's joints are on the rack;
Her corns with shooting pains torment her
And to her bed untimely send her.
Loud quack the ducks, the sea-fowl cry,
The distant hills are looking nigh.
How restless are the snorting swine!
The busy flies disturb the kine.
Low o'er the grass the swallow wings,
The cricket, too, how sharp he sings!
Puss on the hearth, with velvet paws
Sits weeping o'er her whiskered jaws.
The smoke from chimneys right ascends,
Then, spreading, back to earth it bends.
The wind, unsteady, veers around,
Or, settling, in the south is found.
Through the clear stream the fishes rise
And nimbly catch the incautious flies.
The glow-worms, numerous, clear and bright,
Illumed the dewy hill last night.
At dusk the squalid toad was seen,
Like quadruped, stalk o'er the green.
The whirling wind the dust obeys

And in the rapid eddy plays.
The frog has changed his yellow vest
And in a russet coat is dressed.
The sky is green, the air is still,
The mellow blackbird's voice is shrill.
The dog, so altered in his taste,
Quits mutton-bone on grass to feast.
Behold the rooks, how odd their flight,
They imitate the gliding kite
And seem precipitate to fall,
As if they felt the piercing ball.
The tender colts on back to lie,
Nor heed the traveller passing by.
In fiery red the sun doth rise,
Then wades through clouds to mount the skies.
Twill surely rain, we see it with sorrow,
No working in the fields tomorrow.

Having studied the list I can find little fault with it. I wouldn't know about the cricket's call, nor about the glow-worms, which have become rare in southern England. I have always thought that a dog eating grass indicated its instinctive need for medicine, not a change in the weather. And I have my reservations about the lines on the frog and toad. But, by and large, the verses are an accurate account of the signs of rain and show evidence of acute observation.

A P R I L

March winds and April showers
Bring forth May flowers,

is the one piece of April weather lore that everyone knows, and
it is accurate enough.

April weather, rain and sunshine both together, sums up the change-
able nature of spring weather. Rural weather lore is more precise
in its statements:

When April blows his horn
It's good for hay and corn,

refers to thunder in April, for thunder is usually accompanied
by rain, and the general preference is for a wet April:

Betwixt April and May if there be rain
Tis worth more than oxen and wain.

And

April rains for men, May for beasts means that a
rainy April is good but a wet May produces plenty
of grass for cattle.

Again:

> *A cold April the barn will fill* typifies the widespread belief that April should be cold and that therefore cold winds should not be unwelcome.

Concerning some other country sayings we may have our reservations. For instance:

> *A wet Good Friday and a wet Easter Day*
> *Make plenty of grass but very little hay,*

may be a legitimate observation as far as a wet Good Friday is concerned but haymaking depends on the weather in June.

If it rains on Easter Sunday it will rain on every Sunday till Whitsunday, sounds like a generalisation based on a year when every Sunday between Easter and Whitsuntide was wet.

> *If cherries blow in April you'll have your fill,*
> *But if in May, they go away,*

is a doubtful proposition. We are on firmer ground with

> *Till April's dead, change not a thread.*

No-one should think of discarding garments in April, and May is the month to which most of such warnings refer. A couplet widely quoted is:

> *Ash before oak, a regular soak;*
> *Oak before ash, only a splash.*

Unfortunately, an alternative version runs:

> *If the oak comes out before the ash,*
> *We'll have a summer of wet and splash;*

If the ash comes out before the oak,
The summer will be all dust and smoke.

So we may take our choice of the two diametrically opposed proverbs. From my own observation I would say that the oak nearly always comes out before the ash, though sometimes they coincide.

Spring is a fickle season, and April is sometimes one of the harshest months of the year, made more cruel and frustrating by the unwelcome lingering of winter when the warm summer sunshine is so near. In March we have a foretaste of summer, though briefly, but inevitably it is followed by a relapse into wintry conditions. One of the most reliable features of April weather is the intrusion of a 'Blackthorn Winter' towards the end of April, when the blackthorn is in bloom. I remember that some years ago, in the 1950s, I used as a Christmas card a photograph taken in the previous year in my village in Wiltshire. It was one of those sentimental snow scenes which one associates with Christmas, with thatched cottages wearing a thick great-coat of snow and with icicles hanging from the eaves. But it had been taken not on December 25th but on April 25th!

Typical of mid-April weather are small, puffy, white clouds floating on a cold north-easterly breeze over frost-stricken fields. Farmers have been heard to complain bitterly, 'Just as soon as we get the sowing finished and the seed needs warm rain to start it growing, we hit one of these winter droughts.' North Country farmers have a saying, 'As lasting as the parching winds of spring.'

Most country proverbs carry a similar message, warning of the dangers deceived by the early signs of spring:

From Christmas to May weak cattle decay.

Note that it is not until May that any improvements can be relied upon.

In spring, hair is worth more than meat.

That means that no-one can expect a fat animal in spring but that one which has survived the winter by growing a thick coat is likely to do well in the coming summer.

When the cuckoo sings on an empty bough,
Keep your hay and sell your cow.

The empty bough is one without leaves, and one which is in that state by the time the cuckoo arrives indicates a late and backward spring.

If apples bloom in March
In vain you'll for them search;
If apples bloom in April,
Why, then they'll be plentiful;
If apples bloom in May
You may eat them night and day.

Not quite accurate, for an unseasonable frost in May can ruin the apple crop for the year. But the warning is valid enough. Early blooms run greater hazards from frosts.

In most years Easter falls in April, and with it, of course, Good Friday and often Palm Sunday. Good Friday has attracted more than its fair share of rustic lore. If seeds are sown at twelve o' clock on Good Friday the flowers will come up double! Bread made on Good Friday will keep fresh all the year.

Good Friday was widely regarded as the day for planting potatoes, it being held that it was the day *hardained by the Good Lord for plantin' tetties*. This is curious when we consider that the potato has been cultivated in Britain for only about three hundred years. The explanation is probably that Good Friday was one of the few holidays available for the task at the right season, at a time when weekends were not regarded as holidays.

Among the seeds specially mentioned for sowing on Good Friday, which is supposed to germinate very capriciously, is parsley. All will be well, however, if sown on this day; the seedlings will come up without delay, and the leaves will all be curly!

Turning to Easter Sunday, it was a widespread belief that if one rose very early on that morning and climbed to the top of the nearest high hill you could see the sun dance. According to another tradition, a lamb could, with luck, be seen silhouetted against the disc of the rising sun. Many young men and women in times past made the pilgrimage to the top of a high hill in the hope of seeing this phenomenon but usually had their hopes thwarted by cloud.

The weather prophets have naturally been busy with Easter: *Whatever the weather on Easter Day will also prevail at harvest* is a piece of wishful thinking, as is the belief that if the sun shines on Easter Day it will also shine on Whitsunday.

> *A good deal of rain on Easter Day*
> *Gives a good crop of grass but little good hay,*

is more or less repetition of weather lore quoted in March. However, some antiquaries draw attention to the fact that in pagan times there was a tradition of a vernal equinox sacrifice made with a view of ensuring a good harvest, from which these Easter beliefs may have originated.

A white Easter brings a green Christmas is too far-fetched to be valid.

April is the month in which the first cuckoo is heard, and cuckoo lore is abundant:

> *When the cuckoo comes to the bare thorn,*
> *Sell your cow and buy your corn,*

but to it may be added,

> *If the cuckoo sings when the hedge is green,*
> *Keep thy horse and sell thy corn.*

A reasonably reliable piece of country wisdom is: *If it happens to rain for three consecutive days when the cuckoo sings among the oak trees, then late sowing will be as good as early sowing.* Less credible is the belief that the money in your pocket should be turned on hearing the first cuckoo, and the associated saying that it was very unlikely if you had no money in your pocket to turn.

When a girl hears the first cuckoo she kisses her hands and repeats,

> *Cuckoo, cuckoo, when shall I be married?*

The cuckoo replies with its repetitive note, one call for each year of waiting. Older folk asked, instead,

> *Cuckoo, cuckoo, when shall I be released from this world's cares?*

If the cuckoo's first call comes from the right, you will have a prosperous year; if from the left, ill-luck will befall you. And for the best possible luck you should hear the nightingale before the cuckoo.

When you hear the first cuckoo you must drop whatever you are doing and run for a short distance; otherwise you will be lazy all through the year. And whatever you are doing when you hear the first cuckoo, that will be your main occupation during the year ahead.

The well-known verse about the cuckoo rings very true:

> *The cuckoo comes in April,*
> *In May he sings all day,*
> *In June he changes his tune,*
> *In July he prepares to fly,*
> *In August go he must.*

Swallows usually arrive about the middle of April and countrymen consider it lucky to have them nesting on their property, or house-martins under the eaves of their house. The wryneck bears the name of 'the cuckoo's mate', indicating that it was once reasonably common, but it is now very seldom seen. It arrived on migration about five days before the cuckoo.

Of other notable days celebrated in April St. George's Day on April 23rd deserves a mention. In former times blue was the colour worn on that day, to which the following lines refer:

> *On St. George's Day, when blue is worn,*
> *The blue harebell the fields adorn.*

But they are in error. The 'blue harebell' is obviously the blue-bell, which blooms in April, whereas the harebell does not. Though again the verse is misleading, for the harebell is not found in fields but in woods.

Another St. George's Day saying is:

> *When on St. George's Day rye will hide a crow a good*
> *harvest may be expected.*

And

> *On St. George's Day the meadows turn to hay.*

The last three days of March are reputed to be 'borrowed days', borrowed by March from April.

> *March borrows of April*
> *Three days, and they are ill;*
> *April borrows of March again*
> *Three days of wind and rain.*

The significance of this tradition has been forgotten, but it is fact that the last three days are often characterised by a spell of wild, rough weather. And the idea of borrowing days is repeated in the Scottish Highlands by the notion that the first three days of February have been borrowed from January. Again, it has something to do with the weather.

MAY

May has inspired the usual crop of agricultural proverbs, some of them contradictory. *Wet May, long hay*, makes good sense, but I am not so sure about

> *Cold May and windy,*
> *Barn filleth up finely.*

It apparently rests on the assumption that cool and windy weather in May suits corn crops, which, I think, is seldom confirmed by events.

Again,
> *Rain in May*
> *is good for corn and bad for hay.*

I have long been of the opinion that it is impossible to have too much rain in May, the month of growth when all vegetation thrives on frequent showers, and so rain in May should benefit both corn and hay. But I would doubt the truth of the proverb that,

> *A dry May always brings a good crop of wheat.*

Shear your sheep in May
And you'll shear them all away

is a sound warning. Shearing is undertaken not only to take the wool clip but also to help protect the sheep from attacks by flies, which lay their eggs in the wool. There is therefore an incentive to shear early, before flies become too numerous, but it is mistaken enterprise if the sheep take chill in cold, wet weather immediately afterwards. In May we are still in the danger zone for that sort of weather; the best time for shearing sheep is the second week in June, at least in my part of the country.

Who sows in May
Gets little that way

is a proverb relating to oats. Apart from the fact that May is a late date for sowing any kind of cereal, spring-sown oats are very vulnerable to attacks by the frit-fly, at least in southern England, and May is the month when the frit-fly is about. To avoid trouble, oats should be past the four-leaf stage by then.

Ne'er cast a clout
Till May is out

was a rhyme often repeated by solicitous parents in the village of my boyhood, but we were never sure whether the May referred to was the month of May or the hawthorn blossom, which we called May. So we continued to wear our pullovers and flannel vests and thick pants until at least towards the end of the month of May. Which fulfilled the purpose of the proverb in reminding us that, even not that the long-desired month of May had been reached, spring was still fickle and that it was never safe to trust spring weather.

Quite severe frosts sometimes occur in May, even in the south of England. In Devon May 19th, 20th and 21st were once known as Frankimass, the feast of St. Frankan – a saint, incidentally, unknown in any other hagiology. As St. Frankan seems to have been synonymous with the Devil, that is hardly surprising. Frankan was a Devonshire brewer who was meeting with such severe competition from the cider-makers that he sold his soul to the Devil in return for the guarantee of a frost every year on those three days in May, when the apple-trees would be in full bloom. Another version says that as part of the bargain the Devonshire brewers had to agree to adulterate their ale. So when the May frosts come it is a sign that both they and the Devil have been keeping their word!

All this sounds like a bit of anti-brewer propaganda, inspired by Devon cider-makers, but the salient fact is that in most years frosts are to be expected when the apple-trees are in bloom. Fruit farmers have to install elaborate and expensive devices to protect their crops and think themselves lucky when they don't have to use them.

For all that, all over Europe May Day has from very ancient times been celebrated as a spring festival. By May 1st spring has obviously arrived, despite occasional subsequent lapses. The air is filled with bird song; swallows have returned to nest in the barns; bluebells, primroses and wood anenomes are carpeting the woods. (It is worth bearing in mind that before the change in the calendar in 1752 May Day fell eleven days later, and spring would then be even further advanced).

In their origins May Day celebrations may be taken as spontaneous rejoicing over the end of winter and the coming of spring. To our ancestors everything around them spoke of growth and fertility. The new-sown seed was sprouting. Newborn lambs were in the meadows, newly-hatched chicks in the farmyard. New leaves were appearing in the trees. Bees were laying the foundations of new swarms. Birds everywhere were mating and nesting. What could be more natural than for humans to join in?

To rise early on May Day morning and bathe your face in May dew is said to be wonderful for the complexion. In particular, it disperses freckles.

A cottager's proverb, formerly well known, relates to bees:

> *A swarm of bees in May*
> *Is worth a load of hay.*
> *A swarm of bees in June*
> *Is worth a silver spoon.*
> *But a swarm of bees in July*
> *Isn't worth a fly.*

Before beekeepers resorted to the artificial feeding of bees in winter, the bees needed as long a summer as possible to store enough honey to last them through the dark months. That is, those hives which were earmarked for survival, but, of course, it was the custom to destroy the swarms from which honey was collected in autumn, and with these, too, the longer the gathering season the larger the honey store. But a swarm of bees in May is comparatively rare. Its rarity value could indeed perhaps be compared with that of a load of hay.

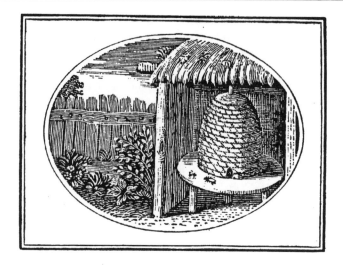

The weather of May attracts its share of country lore.

> *Who doffs his coat on a winter's day*
> *Will gladly put it on in May,*

is, I suppose, a glimpse of the obvious.

> *Look at your corn in May*
> *And you'll come weeping away;*
> *Look at it again in June,*
> *And you'll sing a different tune,*

bears the mark of careful observation. It is surprising how crops improve during the month.

> *Little apples be gone away avore sheep-shearing and*
> *won't be back till harvest.*

refers to the fact that, after the blossom has fallen, it is very difficult to tell whether the fruit has set.

>   *In July, apples go hidey,*

bears the same significance.

>   *A hot May makes a fat churchyard,*
and
>   *For a warm May parsons pray,*

have the same meaning, though without any justification. The latter proverb is probably libellous!

>   *Whoever is ill in the month of May*
>   *For the rest of the year is healthy and gay.*

bears an encouraging message. But who on earth thought up the following saying:

>   *He who bathes in May*
>   *Will soon be laid in clay!*

>   *Fogs in May and heat in June*
>   *Makes the harvest come right soon*

is sound observation.

>   *He that would live for aye*
>   *Must eat sage in May*

sounds a little optimistic, but,

>   *If they would drink nettles in March*
>   *And eat mugwort in May,*
>   *So many fine maidens*
>   *Wouldn't go to the clay,*

bears the same portent.

> *Thunder in May signifieth in that year scarcity,*
> *need dearth of corn and great hunger,*

is full of foreboding, but,

> *The more thunder in May, the less in August and*
> *September,*

sounds more optimistic. To conclude, let me reiterate:

> *The proverbs teach and common people say*
> *It's ill to marry in the month of May!*

It is worth remembering why May is a busy month of traditional festivals and merry-making. The explanation is that May is not only one of the pleasantest and most inspiring months of the year but, in the agricultural calendar, one of the slackest. By the beginning of May, all crops should have been sown. Cows and sheep are grazing in vividly green pastures and require little attention. The lambs are growing but are not yet big enough for slaughter, and the shearing season does not normally begin till June.

Modern gardeners, devoting themselves to exotic crops of which our ancestors knew nothing, find plenty of work to do in May, but for old-time farmers and peasants the month was as near as they could get to a holiday season. What we now regard as the summer holiday period, from mid-July to September, was for them the busiest season of the year – the time of harvest. Even today this apparent reversal of the accepted order still applies to agriculturalists. Few if any farmers could think of taking a holiday between early July and late September, and May is the month in which they can most easily get away from the farm.

There are a few other dates to be ticked off on the calendar for associations with the weather. May 3rd is regarded in Somerset and Devon as Kidney Bean Day, in the belief that they will not grow if planted on any other day. Rain on May 8th foretells a wet harvest. On Ascension Day even a little rain forecasts a season of scarcity ahead and sickness of cattle. On the other hand, if the weather be fine and warm it will remain so until Michaelmas. A bumper corn harvest is sure to follow a fine Whitsunday, but rain encourages the growth of mildew on corn.

JUNE

Agriculturally, June is one of the busier months. The two main activities are haymaking and sheep-shearing (though in the north these two operations are often delayed till July), and there is thus less time for festivals and merrymaking than in May.

Ecclesiastically, too, June is an undistinguished month. Since England became a Protestant country and so lost the feast of Corpus Christi, the chief dates in the Church calendar are Trinity Sunday and the feasts of St. Barnabas, John the Baptist and Peter, though sometimes Whitsuntide falls in June. Trinity Sunday is the Sunday after Whitsunday and has the distinction that the next twenty-seven Sundays are reckoned from it. There are now no other major landmarks in the calendar of the Church of England until we come to Advent, the last Sunday of November.

Most of the weather lore, and folklore in general, of June seems to have clustered around Midsummer Day (June 24th):

> *If it rains on Midsummer Day we may expect a wet harvest.*

If only a little rain falls on this day, corn yields will be indifferent and there will be a poor crop of hazel and walnuts, but apples, pears and plums will give bumper crops. It is widely believed that the best hay is made before Midsummer but that applies only to seeds hay (from crops sown for the purpose) not to meadow hay, which is at its best in July.

> *Barley deserves no praise till after Midsummer Day,*
> *but thereafter it picks up wonderfully.*

> *Cut your thistles before St. John's Day and you'll*
> *have two instead of one,*

is sound advice. And,

> *When the glow-worm lights her lamp,*
> *Then the air is always damp,*

is a bit of original observation.

June is the chief haymaking month, when farmers are preoccupied with getting their hay safely made and stacked. As a country proverb of Devonshire shrewdly points out:

> *Before St. John's we pray for rain; after that we get*
> *it, anyway!*

And now for some weather proverbs:

> *June damp and warm*
> *Does the farmer no harm.*

> *A calm June puts the farmer in tune.*

> *They that go to their corn in May*
> *Come weeping away;*
> *They that go in June*
> *Come back with a merry tune.*
> *A dripping June*
> *Brings all things in tune.*

> *A misty May and a hot June*
> *Bring cheap meal and a harvest soon.*

Likewise:

> *If June be sunny, harvest comes early.*

But

> *A cold and wet June spoils the rest of the year.*

A festival almost forgotten is that of St. Barnabas, June 11th –
an old rhyme:

> *Barnaby bright, Barnaby bright,*
> *The longest day and the shortest night*

is a reminder that, before the change of the calendar in 1752, June
11th *was* the longest day of the year. St. Barnabas is often depic-
ted as carrying a hay-rake, an acknowledgement of the fact that
his day often marks the beginning of haymaking. An old Somerset
proverb says:

> *On St. Barnabas Day mow away – grass or none.*

St. Peter's Day, June 29th, is not forgotten by folklore:

> *If it rains on St. Peter's Day the bakers will have to*
> *carry double flour and single water; if dry, they will*
> *carry single flour and double water.*

And, finally, St. Vitus Day, June 15th:

> *If St. Vitus's Day be rainy weather,*
> *It will rain for thirty days together.*

Prayers used to be offered to St. Vitus that he would use his
influence to prevent rain from spoiling the haymaking.

JULY

July is short of weather lore. In the past our rural ancestors were so preoccupied with the current weather they had little interest in what was going to happen in the coming months.

There are two July days that can be singled out for mention. One is July 6th, Old Midsummer Day (according to the pre-1752 calendar). Just a few old sayings survive:

> *If you hear the cuckoo after Old Midsummer Day*
> *Ere the end of the year your death dues you'll pay.*

The other date in July is St. Swithin's Day, July 15th:

> *St. Swithin's Day if thou dost rain*
> *For forty days it will remain;*
> *St. Swithin's Day if thou be fair,*
> *For forty Days 'twill rain nae mair.*

The saying has its origin in the year 862 when the dying saint, Swithin, requested that his body might be buried in the churchyard at Winchester, 'where the drops of rain might wet his grave'. The monks, however, insisted on burying him in the choir of the cathedral. Whereupon a storm blew up and deluged the procession, and thereafter it rained for forty consecutive days, 'such rain so violent as had never been known'.

A writer in 1920 went to the trouble of examining the rainfall of the previous eighty years and found that there was no record of forty days of rain between July 15th and August 24th. The most occurred in 1895, when rain fell on thirty-four days. And St. Swithin's Day was dry! On the average, only seventeen of the fateful forty days are wet.

More to the point, apples are said to be christened on St. Swithin's Day:

> *Till St. Swithin's Day be past*
> *Apples be not fit to taste.*

When I was at school we believed this and refrained from helping ourselves to apples until the proper date. From that date onwards 'fallers' can be used for making tarts or jam, but our strict interpretation of the calendar was doubtless responsible for many a childhood stomach-ache!

Associated with St. Swithin's Day, doubtless through misinformation about the date, was the saying that if it rained on July 10th it would rain for the next seven weeks! And if it rains on St. Mary's Day (July 2nd) it will rain for a month!

AUGUST

August is the main harvest month in England, when everything gives place to the gathering in of the harvest. Preoccupation with current weather was paramount in everyone's minds, with little time for speculation about the future. An old proverb neatly sums it up:

> *August ripens; September gathers in;*
> *August bears the burden; September the fruit.*

Another carries an admonition:

> *If weather be fair and tidy thy grain,*
> *Make speedy carriage, for fear of rain.*

Few would quarrel with,

> *August sunshine and bright nights ripen the grapes,*

though, as a corrective we might quote:

> *August rain gives honey and wine.*

An observable saying is,

> *After Lammas Day [August 1st] corn ripens by*
> *night as by day.*

There are a few long-term prophecies attached to August, though I attach little credence to them. One is:

> *If the first week of August be warm*
> *The winter will be white and long.*

And likewise:

> *A fog in August indicates a severe winter and*
> *plenty of snow.*

> *As August, so next February,*

sounds precise, but I suspect that by next February everyone will have forgotten the weather of August.

Summing up the successful year is the rhyme:

A frosty winter, and a dusty March,
And a rain about April
and another about Lammas-time;
When the corn begins to fill,
A pint of rain is worth a pot of gold.

There is a good deal of weather lore associated with St. Bartholomew's Day (August 24th). It is said that

St. Bartholomew's mantle wipes dry all the tears
St. Swithin can cry,

a reference to the fact that the forty days from St. Swithin's are up on St. Bartholomew's.

If August 24th be fair and clear,
Then hope for a prosperous autumn that year,

is reinforced by

As St. Bart's Day, so the autumn.

Another has it that *should the morning begin with a hoar frost, then cold weather can soon be expected and a hard winter,* but I would think that a hoar frost on August 24th is an unlikely event.

For some reason there are three days of the year which, since Saxon times, have been termed 'Egyptian Days', when bad luck holds sway. One of these is the second Monday of August. The first is the last Monday in April, but I have been unable to discover what is the third. There is a suggestive entry in the Anglo-Saxon Chronicle for the year 1116:

> *This was a very vexatious and destructive year with respect to the fruits of the earth, through the immoderate rains that fell soon after the beginning of August, harassing and perplexing men till Candlemas Day.*

And in the following year:

> *This was a very blighted year for corn, through the rains that scarcely ceased for nearly all the year.*

Did the writer of the Chronicle have in mind the killing of William Rufus, whose mysterious death in the New Forest on August 2nd, 1100, was widely held to have been an act of ritual sacrifice to the old gods? Was it a monastic protest against a pagan superstition that had a strong hold on the minds of the people?

Lammas Day, or more particularly Lammas Day (Old Style) which is August 12th by the present calendar, was the occasion of many fairs and associated festivities throughout Britain. The event is perpetuated by the date being a convenient one for early sheep fairs. Manx folklore suggests that there were, in Celtic mythology, two gods of harvest – an older god named Crom Dubh and a younger one, Lugh (apparently a sun god), who forced Crom Dubh to yield the harvest from the dark and reluctant earth. The story introduces an element of conflict and hence an occasion for rejoicing and celebration when the 'goodie' wins. But this is only incidentally related to the weather.

SEPTEMBER

Weather lore for September tends to be concentrated around Michaelmas. Fair weather on Michaelmas Day was held to betoken a fine but cold winter, though a proverb current in Berkshire stated, *A dark Michaelmas, a light Christmas.*

There were said to be three days in the middle of September (the actual dates being variable, though usually the 20th to the 22nd) which determined the weather for the next three months. If warm with a south wind, the next three months would experience similar weather; if wet or stormy, the next three months would be cloudy. Another version says that the three days should always be windy, and if they are not the ensuing winter will compensate for them by being unusually rough. In Cornwall the critical date is October 10th – Michaelmas (Old Style):

> *As many days old as the moon is on Michaelmas*
> *Day, so many floods shall we have after.*
>
> *If St. Michael brings many acorns Christmas will*
> *cover the fields with snow.*

On neither of these proverbs do I feel competent to pass an opinion. However, the saying that if you eat goose on Michaelmas Day you will never want money the year round has the merit of being based on common sense. For by Michaelmas if the year has gone well there should be a fat goose available for dinner. The saying is versified in the proverb,

> *September, when by custom (right Divine),*
> *Geese are ordained to bleed at Michael's shrine.*

Another interpretation, slightly different, is put on the custom in the lines:

> *When tenanntes come to pay their quarter's rent*
> *They bring some fowle at Mid-summer, a dish of fish*
> *at Lent,*
> *At Christmas a capon, at Michaelmas a goose,*
> *And something else at New Year's-tide, for feare their*
> *lease flies loose.*

And another rhyme carries the same message:

> *The custom came up from the tenants presenting*
> *Their landlords with geese, to incline their relenting*
> *On following payments ...*

In some districts the feast of St. Matthew, September 21st, was known as 'The Devil's Nutting Day'; in others, the epithet belonged to Holy Rood Day (September 14th); but in yet others the taboo against gathering nuts applied to every Sunday. Most widespread of all beliefs is that the Devil spits (or, in a more precise version, urinates) on blackberries on a certain date in autumn, rendering them unfit to eat. Michaelmas Day is often quoted, though some have thought that Old Michaelmas Day is intended. It is true, however, that, as autumn goes on, frost and more particularly maggot-producing flies have usually spoiled most of the blackberry crop. I think that I would not gather blackberries for culinary purposes after Michaelmas.

Here are a few more weather proverbs concerned with the month of September as a whole:

> *Fair on the first of September, fair for the whole month.*

> *The more thunder in May, the less in August and September.*

> *A wet June makes a dry September.*

> *A cherry year, a merry year;*
> *A plum year, a dumb year.*

> *September blow soft*
> *Till the fruit's in the loft*

is by way of being an admonition. And

> *Good harvests make men prodigal, bad ones provident,*

is a piece of acute observation.

St. Matthew's Day (September 22nd) is one of three days in the month which rule the weather for October, November and December. A south wind on September 21st indicates that the rest of the autumn will be warm:

> *St. Matthew's Day, bright and clear,*
> *Brings good wine in next year.*

St. Matthew, shut up the bee, means that bee-hives are closed for the winter. But I am at a loss to suggest the meaning of *St. Matthew brings on the cold dew.*

Paradoxically, of course, the weather plays a preponderant role in almost every farming activity in September. With the late harvest still to be gathered and every day reducing the chances of winning it in good condition, every farmer on waking in the morning casts his weather eye at the clouds and estimates the chances of a fine day ahead. Some weather signs are entirely reliable:

> *Evening red and morning grey,*
> *Two good signs for a fine day.*
> *Evening grey and morning red*
> *Send the farmer wet to bed.*

> *Grey mists at dawn,*
> *the day will be warm,*

and,

> *Dew in the night,*
> *Next day will be bright*

are both accurate. Rising in the morning to find it raining by no means discourages the knowledgeable farmer, who appreciates that

> *Rain before seven –*
> *Fine before eleven.*

Also,

> *A sun-shiny shower won't last half-an-hour.*

When the weather is about to change for the worst the following rhyme applies:

> *Long foretold, long last;*
> *Short notice, soon past.*

> *If the sun goes pale to bed,*

it is a bad sign for the weather on the morrow.

> *Smoke falling instead of rising;*
> *Soot falling down the chimney;*
> *The blacksmith's anvil sweating,*

are all reliable signs of rain.

And

> *Rain from the East*
> *Will last three days at least.*

Similarly,

> *When the wind is in the East*
> *Tis neither good for man nor beast.*

But,

> *When the wind is in the West,*
> *Then the wind is at its best.*

The wise farmer studies the clouds. A mackerel sky is mottled like a fish and when it appears foretells stormy weather:

> *Mackerel sky, mackerel sky,*
> *Never long wet or dry.*

Chunky clouds indicate showery weather, and

> *A rain-topped cloud with flattened base*
> *Carries rain-drops on its face,*

but,

> *If woolly fleeces strew the heavenly way,*
> *Be sure no rain disturbs the summer day.*

Although there is controversy about the extent to which the moon influences the weather, the appearance of the moon offers a useful guide. A watery moon, when the moon shines weakly through high clouds, indicates rain, as does also a halo round the moon. When you see the old moon in the young moon's arms, meaning when the old moon appears as a dark shadow above the new moon, it forecasts a fine day. Some countrymen believe that the weather on the first day of the new moon indicates what it will be for the rest of the month, but I have never found this very reliable.

Rooks are good weather forecasters. When on leaving their nest they fly straight to their foraging grounds the day will be fine. If they twist and turn rough weather is on the way, and they will not venture far from their nests or roosts when a gale threatens. This is understandable, as the rook is not particularly strong on the wing and it doesn't like being caught out at a distance from home by a sudden gale.

When swallows and swifts fly high the weather will be fine. This is because they are pursuing gnats, flies and other insects which react to high barometric pressure. Similarly they fly low when the barometer is low.

Blackbirds and robins, among other birds, perch high for their morning song if there is promise of a fine day but lower in the tree when rain threatens. The skylark in fine weather takes its time over its descent from its song flight, hovering and gliding, but when rain is imminent it drops straight to the ground. The green woodpecker is another bird whose loud 'yaffling' is considered a sign of rain.

With the development of inland reservoirs and sewage farms gulls have changed their habitats. Early this century to see a gull inland indicated rough weather; now they are regular visitors to inland sites. Except during the breeding season, when for three or four months they are seldom or never seen inland except in spells of bad weather. To see a gull inland during these months is a sure sign of rain and gales.

Most dogs have knowledge of an approaching thunderstorm before it can be detected by humans. Their reaction varies from a vague unease to sheer panic. Pigs also become very restless when gales threaten and wander around their sties, carrying straw in their mouths. Old countrymen swear that pigs can see the wind. You detect a sign of approaching rain by observing the direction goats are facing when grazing. If they are facing the wind the weather will be fine, but if they graze with their tail towards the wind, rain will follow.

When cows linger in the vicinity of their cowshed or stand with their tails towards the wind, rain is imminent:

> *When a cow tries to scratch its ear,*
> *Then a shower is very near.*

Cats become restless and frequently wash behind their ears when the weather is about to change from 'set fair' to 'gales'. Spiders stand at their front door, looking out to see the approaching rain. They spin their long gossamer strands only when they are assured of a spell of fine weather.

Bees are a reliable guide to the weather:

> *When the bees crowd out of their hive*
> *The weather makes it good to be alive:*
> *But when the bees crowd into their hive again*
> *Beware the rapid approach of rain.*

Many flowers close their petals when rain threatens; daisies and dandelions are readily observable. But the most reliable is the scarlet pimpernel, which infallibly shuts up shop on the approach of rain.

There are many more aids to weather forecasting in other seasons of the year, but I have been content to quote those which help the farmer anxious to get his precious harvest in store before the weather breaks and autumn storms predominate. September is a notable month for fairs, notably sheep fairs, but pleasant as they can be when the sun shines they are held on the appointed date, come gales, rain or thunder.

OCTOBER

By October autumn has settled in, harvest is over, and ploughing is proceeding apace. The weather lore for the month is mostly devoted to predictions of the prospects for the coming winter. Here are some of them:

Much rain in October, much wind in December.

Ice in October to bear a duck,
Nothing afterwards but slush and muck.

The same rhyme, however, is recited about November:

If the deer's coat is grey in October there will be a
severe winter.

This is a saying current in Exmoor, where presumably it is based on observation. Frost is not often a prolonged feature in October – three frosts and then rain – but in the year 789 a frost which began on October 1st lasted until February 26th of the next year.

In October manure your field,
And your land its wealth shall yield,

is sound advice.

Dry your barley in October
Or you'll always be sober

is a reminder that if this is not done there will be no malt and therefore no opportunity to get drunk!

If it should freeze or snow in October, January will be mild, but for every fog in October there will be snow in winter. If when the leaves are falling in October many of them wither on the tree and hang there, it foretells a frosty winter and much snow. Note the full moon in October; if it comes without frost there will be no frost until the full moon in November.

A good October and a good blast
To blow the hog acorns and mast.

In other words, October should provide a good, strong wind to blow the acorns and beech-mast off the trees so that the pigs may feed on them.

Cuckoo wheat and woodcock hay
Will make a farmer run away.

'Cuckoo wheat' is wheat sown in April; 'woodcock hay' is hay made in October; both dates too late to be of much use.

When the horn of the huntsman is heard on the hill
It is time for the farmer to look for his drill.

In short, hunting and the drilling of autumn wheat should coincide.

Late fruit keeps well.

St. Luke's Day, October 18th, has its associations with weather lore in the term 'St. Luke's Little Summer', which refers to a spell of fine, sunny weather that often occurs around this time. In some parts of the country the belief is applied to Martinmas, the period being known as 'St. Martin's Little Summer', but that is less appropriate, November 11th (St. Martin's Day) being rather late.

Hallowe'en at the end of October marked the end of harvest and the beginning of the gloomy reign of winter. The winter fires, which burned on the hearth all through the dark months, were kindled. Surplus animals were slaughtered and salted down for winter use.

NOVEMBER

St. Martin's Day, or Martinmas (November 11th), is the date in November which has attracted most weather lore. As recorded under October, cattle and sheep were brought in from the hills and housed for the winter, the surplus being slaughtered, as were pigs. Early in the present century, when I was a boy, the cottage pig was a feature of many village cottages, and November was the month of its demise. My father was the parish pig-killer and was always busy throughout the month. For a few weeks everyone feasted on chitterlings, faggots and other delicacies, while flitches of bacon and hams were salted down and stored on racks in the kitchen or in the open chimney for use during the winter.

Regarding weather lore, All Saints's Day is supposed to bring a 'little summer', a continuance of St. Luke's Little Summer, which brings three days of glorious weather. This is the date on which West Country farmers began cider-making.

> *On the 1st of November, if the weather hold clear*
> *An end of wheat sowing do make for the year,*

is good advice, though much wheat is now sown a little later.

And there is much common sense in the lines:

> *Set trees at Allhallowtide and command them to prosper;*
> *Set them after Candlemas and entreat them to grow.*

There is a country saying that:

> *As the season for apples and other fruit comes to an*
> *end, so the stains made by the juices on cloth will*
> *disappear,*

but I have never noticed the truth of this:

> *Thunder in November, a bountiful year to follow.*

But thunder in November is very rare.

> *A wet November, a plentiful year*

has more chance of being correct.

> *A snow year, a rich year,*

promises well and compensates for the advice,

When frost and snow come both together,
Sit by the fire and spare shoe leather.

If ducks do slide at Hallowe'en
At Christmas they will swim;
If ducks do swim at Hallantide,
At Christmas they will slide;

but the link between the two types of weather is seldom as clearcut.

If on All Saints' Day the beech nut is dry, we shall
a hard winter, but if the nut be wet we may expect
a wet winter,

but in many years there are not enough beech-nuts to test this formula.

St. Martin's Day is associated with a last taste of summer:

Another spell of glorious sun
Should with St. Martin's season come.

St. Martin's summer means a warm month,

and

If the wind is in the south-east at Martinmas it will
remain there till after Christmas.

Though another version says that if the wind is SSW at Martinmas it will keep mainly to the same quarter till Old Candlemas Day (February 14th), and the winter up to that date will be mild, with virtually no snow. If at Martinmas it is dry and cold, the cold in the coming winter will not last long.

November 23rd is St. Clement's Day, notable because St. Clement is the patron saint of blacksmiths, who held a festival to mark the occasion. The weather lore for this day is that as it is fair or foul so it will be next February.

November was the month when threshing began, when this was done by flail. From this time onwards the air in villages and around farmsteads was never silent by day.

In November the trees shed their leaves, usually in the following order: Walnut, sycamore, horse chestnut, lime, ash; then elm; then beech and oak; then apple (sometimes not till the end of November); and lastly young beeches and pollarded oaks, which may retain their withered leaves till pushed off by the new ones in spring.

Finally, let me quote a favourite rhyme of mine:

> *If you wed in bleak November,*
> *Only joy will come, remember.*

I was married on November 1st, and my wife and I celebrated our golden wedding in November 1989.

DECEMBER

Weather lore is almost embarrassingly abundant for December. It falls naturally between that applicable to the whole month and that which is concentrated on certain dates in the month, notably Christmas. As December holds the shortest day of the year, it is only natural to look for signs of what the coming year will serve up.

> *A good winter brings a good summer,*

but that depends on what we consider makes a good winter. Many would be inclined to the view that

> *He that passeth a winter's day escapes an enemy.*

> *Winter finds out what summer lays up ,*

is a statement of the obvious.

> *A green winter makes a fat churchyard,*

but so does any sort of winter.

Concerning December thunder there are conflicting proverbs:

> *Winter's thunder and summer's flood*
> *Never boded Englishmen good;*

but

> *Thunder in December foretells fair weather.*

For all that, thunder in December is rare.

Cold with snow is said to be good for rye, and a snow year will be a rich year. An unusually fine and mild day in winter is sometimes called a 'Borrowed Day'. It has to be repaid with interest a little later on!

Nearly all the lore attached to the winter solstice, however, has accrued to Christmas.

> *Light Christmas, light wheatsheaf;*
> *Dark Christmas, heavy wheatsheaf,*

and in this context 'light' and 'dark' are supposed to refer to the new or full moon.

If Christmas comes during the waxing moon we shall have a

very good year; but if during a waning moon, a hard year. And the nearer to the end of the moon, the worse the year will be.

> *If the sun shines through the apple-tree on Christmas*
> *Day, the apple-trees will bear much fruit.*

The same is true if it is windy on Christmas Day. If it snows during Christmas night the crops will do well, and if at Christmas ice hangs on the willow, clover may be cut at Easter. Thunder during Christmas week (an unlikely event) indicates that there will be much snow during the winter. If the ice will bear a duck at Christmas it won't bear a mouse afterwards.

> *If Christmas Day on a Sunday fall*
> *A troublous winter we shall have all,*

but

> *If Christmas Day on a Monday be*
> *A great winter that year you'll see.*

To return to agricultural lore, you should plant shallots on the shortest day and harvest them on the longest.

> *If New Year's Eve night the wind blow south,*
> *It betokeneth warmth and growth;*
> *If west, much milk and fish in the sea;*
> *If north much cold and storms there will be;*
> *If east, the trees will bear much fruit;*
> *If north-east, flee it, man and brute.*

To conclude, here is a rhyme taught to Somerset children a hundred years ago:

January falls the snow;
February cold winds blow;
In March peep out the early flowers;
And April comes with sunny showers;
In May the roses bloom so gay;
In June the farmer mows his hay;
In July brightly shines the sun;
In August harvest is begun;
September turns the green leaves brown;
October winds then shake them down;
November fills with bleak and smear;
December comes and ends the year.

WEATHER RECORDS

Almost every year some weather record is broken. In my book *Agricultural Records* I compiled weather records from about the year 220 to 1977, and the results were very revealing. 1977 had a typical weather pattern, but it was the only one in recent times that did not break some weather record or other.

In 1976:
'Authorities were faced with unprecedented conditions.'
'The drought record beginning in May 1875 can confidently be assessed as the worst on record for a sixteen-month period as far back as quantitative comparisons are available for England and Wales.'

1975 was the fifth driest year on the century.

1974: 'Last autumn was the fifth wettest on record for this century.'

1973 brought the 'least rainfall in England and Wales since 1964.'

1972 was 'Scotland's driest since 1955.'

1971 rainfall 'was well below average.'

In 1970 it is recorded that 'the six-year period 1965-1970 is the wettest on record since 1927-32.'

1969 'for the fifth consecutive year rainfall was greater than average.'

1968 produced 'the wettest summer since 1931.'

In 1967 the rainfall was 'greater than average for the third consecutive year.'

1966 produced a weather pattern which was one of the wettest years on the century.

And three years earlier, 1963, had an exceptionally severe winter, when snow which fell on Boxing Day was still lying on the ground on March 11th.

Over the preceding sixteen years warm, dry summers alternated with cool, rainy ones, but 1947 produced very severe weather, with much snow and prolonged frost, in the early months of the year. In the blizzards from January 23rd to the middle of March about six million sheep and some 30,000 store cattle perished.

Since then there have been a number of years characterised by dry, warm summers, giving rise to predictions of global warming and a new era of subtropical summers, both from amateur forecasters and from scientists who might be supposed to know better. But the records reveal that there is nearly always something exceptional about the British weather. And always has been.

Let us look back even farther. 1924 was one of the wettest years on record, when seven consecutive months, from April to October, all had above average rainfall. 1921 produced the driest June since records were kept, and February was not much better. In 1916 violent gales with tremendous downpours caused flooding, and June was the coldest for fifty years. 1911 gave absolute drought in July, August and early September, the temperature reaching 100°F at Greenwich on August 9th. In 1899 another hot, dry summer, gave one of the earliest harvests on record. And the notable feature of 1881 was the worst snowstorm of the nineteenth century, on January 18th and 19th. Piling up immense drifts, it brought all business to a standstill and caused much loss of life.

So the saga goes on. The writer of the Biblical Book of Ecclesiastes was right when he said:

> The thing that hath been, it is that which shall be;
> and that which is done is that which shall be done;
> and there is no new thing under the sun. Is there
> anything whereof it may be said, See, this is new?
> It hath been already of old time ...

However, there are long-term, very long-term, weather patterns which may be detected. One of the most plausible is that postulated by the late Professor Otto Pettersson, who spent a lifetime studying the ocean currents that fluctuated through the channels which feed the Baltic Sea. He finds abundant evidence of a cycle of eighteen centuries:

> A period of deteriorating weather began in the
> twelfth or thirteenth centuries, when settlements
> in Greenland began to be abandoned in the face
> of advancing ice. The entire Baltic was frozen over,
> the sea-coast of Holland was inundated by disas-
> trous floods, famine is increasingly quoted as
> occurring in all the countries of Europe, including
> Britain. Eighteen centuries from that period would
> bring us to the year 31000, when a further era of
> ice and storm may be expected.

But since that last visitation, which lasted for several centuries, our climate has been steadily improving. And it will continue to do so until at least the twenty-second century. Our grandchildren will have a respite throughout their lifetime! After that, the climate will start to deteriorate again.

Meantime other evidence all points towards the conclusion

that the northern hemisphere is warming up. Sea temperatures along the coast of Norway have been growing warmer since 1920. Cod fisheries have shifted steadily northwards. Summer bird visitors press farther into the Arctic and in greater numbers as the years pass. The glaciers of the Alps, Alaska and even of the high mountains of East Africa are shrinking.

Yet although this is the overall pattern of climatic events, there is no foundation for the exercise of attempting to formulate short-term weather forecasts from it. Let us look at the year 1348, when the Black Death came to England. That year comes when the deterioration of the climate was well advanced, and, sure enough, the records speak of

> An excessively wet summer, with almost continuous rain from midsummer to Christmas. Serious floods followed, and much of the harvest was not gathered. The Black Death caused very heavy mortality.

Yet of the previous four years, three were years of drought and produced good harvests!

Many medieval years are recorded as 'years of famine'. 1315 is stated to have been

> the first year of the great famine. It is said that the crops in England were almost a total failure ... There was heavy mortality among human beings and cattle, and the situation was aggravated by plague among cattle.

But by 1332 the record is of 'an excellent harvest and general prosperity in the countryside.'

There was a period of poor harvests from 1527 to 1534, when the Thames was frozen in London and to some miles below Gravesend, but from 1535 to 1543 there followed a series of abundant harvests. In 1684 an exceptionally severe spell of cold weather began in December, 1683, and continued for the first eight weeks of 1684:

> The river was quite frozen over by January 9th and streets of booths were set up on the Thames. By the 16th the shopping streets stretched from bank to bank, and horses, carts and coaches crossed over on the ice. Printing presses were set up to print, as souvenirs, cards giving the name of the person who bought them, the date and the year, and the fact that they were printed on the ice on the Thames.

Yet the next year was characterised by a summer, autumn and early winter that were warm and wet.

Again, the year 1740, the beginning of a spell of four exceptionally dry years, saw a Frost Fair on the Thames from Christmas, 1739, to February 17th, 1740:

> Many hens and ducks, even cattle in the stalls, died of cold; trees split asunder. Not only beer but wine in cellars froze. Deeply sunken wells were covered with impenetrable ice. Crows and other birds fell to the ground, frozen in their flight. No bread was eatable, for it was as cold and hard as a stone.

The harvest suffered, but in the next year it had recovered, for 'the harvest was abundant and gathered in good order. Beef was sold for a penny a pound, and wheat for sixpence a stone ...'

According to Professor Pettersson, there are lesser rhythmically occurring periods that fall at intervals, namely, every nine, eighteen and thirty-six years. I have checked this statement and find nothing to substantiate it. There is nothing to be gained by trying to predict the weather, except in the broadest terms, by studying records of the past.

Some titles from the COUNTRY BOOKSHELF:

LETTERS FROM THE ENGLISH COUNTRYSIDE
Ralph Whitlock
158 pages; illustrated with pen & ink drawings; Price £4.95

O WHO WILL MARRY ME? *A Book of Country Love*
Ralph Whitlock; *80 pages; illustrated with Bewick engravings;*
Price £3.50

**GRAN'S OLD-FASHIONED REMEDIES, WRINKLES
AND RECIPES,** *and*
GRAN'S OLD-FASHIONED GARDENING GEMS
Jean Penny
Charmingly illustrated with period engravings; Price £3.50 each

MAISIE AND ME: *A Country Childhood in the 1920s*
Stella Ashton; *80 pages, pen & ink drawings, £3.95*

WINIFRED: *Her Childhood and early working life*
Sylvia Marlow; *128 pages; Illustrated throughout; Price £4.50*

The **ROMANY WAY**
Irene Soper; *112 pages; Fully Illustrated; Price £4.95*

LAND GIRL: *Her Story of six years in the Women's Land
Army, 1940-46* by Anne Hall
144 pages; Illustrated throughout; Price £4.95

LUMBER JILL: *Her Story of four years in the Women's Timber
Corps*
Mavis Williams; *96 pages; Illustrated; Price £3.95*

*Ex Libris Press books may be obtained through your local book-
shop or direct from the publisher, post-free, on receipt of net price,
at: 1 The Shambles, Bradford on Avon, Wiltshire, BA15 1JS.
Please ask for our free, illustrated catalogue of around 50 titles.*